# YOUR KNOWLEDGE HAS VALUE

- We will publish your bachelor's and master's thesis, essays and papers

- Your own eBook and book - sold worldwide in all relevant shops

- Earn money with each sale

Upload your text at www.GRIN.com and publish for free

**Peter Becker**

**Well-meant is the enemy of the good. Western good governance concepts and the reality in developing countries**

GRIN Publishing

**Bibliographic information published by the German National Library:**

The German National Library lists this publication in the National Bibliography; detailed bibliographic data are available on the Internet at http://dnb.dnb.de .

**Imprint:**

Copyright © 2015 GRIN Verlag, Open Publishing GmbH
Print and binding: Books on Demand GmbH, Norderstedt Germany
ISBN: 978-3-668-01321-6

**This book at GRIN:**

http://www.grin.com/en/e-book/301649/well-meant-is-the-enemy-of-the-good-western-good-governance-concepts-and

**GRIN - Your knowledge has value**

Since its foundation in 1998, GRIN has specialized in publishing academic texts by students, college teachers and other academics as e-book and printed book. The website www.grin.com is an ideal platform for presenting term papers, final papers, scientific essays, dissertations and specialist books.

**Visit us on the internet:**

http://www.grin.com/

http://www.facebook.com/grincom

http://www.twitter.com/grin_com

# Well-meant is the enemy of the good

Western good governance concepts and the reality in developing countries

**Peter Becker**

**About the author:**

Peter Becker is lawyer, political scientist and economist and has
worked as an advisor in the sector of good governance for more the nine
years in Indonesia, Cambodia and Cameroon. Back in Germany he is
teaching constitutional law at the University of applied sciences of
Public Administration Police and Judicature in Güstow but is still
engaged at the National University of Management, Phnom Penh and
the I. Arabev State University, Bishkek.

## INTRODUCTION

*This paper is meant as a contribution to the discussion of the effectiveness of development aid. Since the last decade of the 20th century Western industrialized countries have undertaken encompassing efforts to improve government systems in developing countries because bad government is seen as one of the most serious hurdles for prosperity and poverty alleviation. Billions of dollars have been spent in order to fight corruption and nepotism, and to foster democracy and the rule of law. But already a brief glance at the history of developing countries in the last 25 years shows that much of this support has mostly not given rise to any substantial ameliorations, and in those regions where prosperity was achieved the success cannot be traced back to Western good governance programs. This article [1] demonstrates in particular why one of the most popular development aid instruments in context of good governance programs - decentralization reform - is doomed to fail.*

---

[1] This article is the resume of three of the author's books about the decentralization and the political system in Cambodia and Cameroon written in German: *Dezentralisierung in Kambodscha. Anspruch und Wirklichkeit ambitiöser Entwicklungsvorhaben, 2014, LIT-Verlag, Transformationsziel Demokratie. Zivilgesellschaft und Dezentralisierung in Kamerun, 2014, Universitätsverlag Potsdam (together with Alexander Kopp); Rechenschaftspflichten und Dezentralisierung in Kamerun. Westliche Konzepte und afrikanische Ideen, 2014,.LIT-Verlag*

# Table of Contents

## I. A brief history of Western good governance programs

As the German scholar Ulrich Menzel has pointed out in his book chapter on the theory of development [2] , for most of the time human development was primarily conceived as a purely economic process. As a consequence Western development aid, which was created in the aftermath of the Second World War as a kind of global "Marshall Plan" for colonial states on their way to independence, initially was understood as a means to support economic progress in less developed countries. The lack of success of the development assistance programs of the 1960s and 1970s, and the debt crisis in developing countries which emerged in the 1980s, however, pointed clearly to a strong correlation between economic achievements and the overall policy framework. As a consequence the World Bank and the IMF administered structural adjustment programs for highly indebted Third World countries in order to replace the exuberant and ineffective state structures by market mechanisms. However, these programs did not achieve the desired results.

But things changed again when in 1989 the report "Sub-Saharan Africa: From Crisis to Sustainable Growth," commissioned by the World Bank, was published. The main conclusion of this

---

[2] Menzel, 2010.

5

report was that Africa's development problems are not so much caused by the poverty of the African States. The report stated that they are rather the result of a "Crisis of Governance," in particular the consequence of too powerful elites, corruption, abuse of power and violent conflict resolution. Thereby it became clear that the solution was not simply to downsize the government apparatus in favor of free market mechanisms. A state able to provide reliable institutions (in the sense of "rules of the game") which are necessary to run a functioning market economy, in short the "capable state," became the new goal. The governance model of the capable state was initially understood as a purely technical concept. However, soon it was tied to the call for human rights, the rule of law and democratic reforms, and by adding the adjective "good" to the term of governance, it was transformed into a normative concept.

After the collapse of the Soviet Union, the calls of Western states on governments in developing countries for a policy according to this concept of good governance became more intense due to the fact that their risk of drifting into the Communist camp was now banished. Moreover, this occurred at the same time that industrialized countries felt they were in position as the sole financier of development aid. Western development bureaucracy tried to size this hour. Suddenly it seemed to them that it might be possible not only to foster industrial production or the construction of hospitals, or to support the training of workers or doctors. By the means of development assistance, also fighting against authoritarian and repressive regimes in the beneficiary countries, identified as a major obstacle to development, seemed to be feasible. The Paris Declaration from 2005 officially turned the development aid system of the past into a development cooperation where donor and receiver countries are considered to be development partners. The idea behind this move was to grant development aid on the basis of mutual contracts under which governments in developing countries agree to conduct good governance reforms in exchange for financial support. It was assumed that Third World country governments would be interested in Western aid programs, because the aid could help to improve the welfare of the population and in this way, contribute to the stabilization of their regimes. In addition, a system of so called "conditionalities," linked to aid programs, was sought to make even authoritarian and repressive ruling governments willing to conduct democratic reforms and to adopt the principles of the rule of law. The term "conditionalities" refers to a system of mechanisms starting from special incentives up to sanctions, such as reducing support or the termination of the cooperation.[3]

But was it really realistic to believe that the prospect of receiving some donor money would

---

[3] Further details: Becker, 2014a; Kielwein, 2007.

change the mindsets of the leaders of "bad" governments who have made it a policy – in some cases over decades – to channel the country's revenues into their own pockets and accumulate a fortune of billions of US$? Was it likely that civil servants in these countries, who have benefited from this kind of governance and have been shaped over decades by practicing corruption and embezzling public monies, suddenly will stick to the principles of the rule of law? And perhaps even more serious, can we assume that a population, badly educated and mostly living in tribal structures without any experience in the rules of democracy and any perceptions of modern law, will be able to take over the role as an electorate that can effectively control the government? In contrast Singapore, Taiwan, South Korea, Malaysia and Thailand for example, where a phenomenal economic growth occurred after the Second World War and lifted the quality of living close to European standards, entered the development race with nothing more than the human capital of their population and the spirit of their leaders, but neither under a democratic rule nor with the helping hand of Western good governance programs.[4]

Looking at these questions from the perspective of a Western adviser and counsel in Indonesia, Cambodia and Cameroon for more the 9 years, my answer is clearly "no." But the answer "no"

---

[4] Fukuyama, 1992, p. 101

also admits that there is a wide gulf between the objectives and the reality of the current Western good governance programs. The following analysis has the details.

## II. Criticism of development aid and the evaluation problem

The US President Harry S. Truman stated in a famous speech in 1949: *"More than half the people of the world are living in conditions approaching misery. Their food is inadequate. They are victims of disease. Their economic life is primitive and stagnant. Their poverty is a handicap and a threat both to them and to more prosperous areas. For the first time in history, humanity possesses the knowledge and skill to relieve the suffering of these people."* It is assumed that this speech was the starting point for modern Western development aid and remains still its justification and guideline. Hence, it is safe to say that the main objective of development aid or nowadays "development cooperation" is to improve the standard of living of the population by fostering the development of their countries. This means bringing democracy and the rule of law to developing countries cannot be the final objective of development cooperation, and it is of course up to the people of every country to decide whether they prefer to live in a liberal democracy or not. Democracy and the rule of law are at best only stages of a path which the majority of Western societies believe will lead to economic prosperity, but without having clear evidence for this assumption.[5] But development bureaucracies obviously have lost sight of the ultimate goal and tend to apply the maxim of Confucius "the journey is the reward" instead. Therefore the idea of good governances has become an end in its own right. This results frequently in development aid programs designed to install government concepts and practices in the Third World which might have stood the test of time in the OECD-world but hardly fit societies in countries with totally different historical and cultural backgrounds and stages of development.

Amazingly, precisely those donors and development bureaucrats, preaching the concept of good governance, don't like to listen to such critics when it comes to their own system of governance. It is undeniable that the number of voices, claiming on the basis of different arguments that this kind of aid has no sustainable impact on poverty but tends to stabilize corrupt government regimes, has mounted during recent years increasingly. However, among development bureaucrats we can only observe a strong tendency to follow the

---

[5] Fukuyama has already in 1992 in a convincing and comprehensive way demonstrated that democracy is not a precondition for prosperity. As countries like China, Taiwan Singapore, South Korea or even the Soviet Union (until the end of the 1960th) indicate, up to a certain level of development authoritarian regimes have huge advantages by fostering economic growth (Fukuyama, 1992, S. 124 et seq.).

motto "let's close our eyes and ears and press on." This is why for people who wish to do an honest job in context of development cooperation, the question becomes more and more pressing, whether current Western-funded governance projects are really able to improve the living situation of the poor or have become entirely a nice playground for donor organizations and their employers. Brigitte Erler in her book "The Deadly Aid" [6] had asserted already in 1983 that development aid is obviously doing more bad than good. But a good answer to the question, what precisely goes wrong with good governance programs, is hard to find. Is it only the single project that fails? Is it the weakness or incompetence of donor organizations to implement good governance programs? Or has the whole concept proven to be unsuitable to developing countries?

Composing an essay to give a satisfying explanation is a more complicated undertaking than it seems at first glance. The main reason is a certain "micro-macro-puzzle."[7] If we try to look at the problem from the macro perspective it is practically impossible to trace back the chain between the activities and the impacts of a single good governance program activity due to the complexity of society. For example, we can look into statistics about the national or regional

---

[6] Erler, 2003.
[7] Merkel, 2010, p. 467 et seq.

poverty rate or the education level, or in reports about the accessibility and quality of the health service. But even if these figures are reliable and point to improvements, the correlation between these factors and the program activities remains widely unclear. On the other hand, if we try to look at the results of certain activities at the spot, the conclusions we are able to draw from our findings will be very limited and will not allow us to judge the impact of poverty-relevant political or social changes on the macro-level. Therefore the results of evaluation reports which frequently try to follow impact chains are in most cases completely based on speculations.[8] Hence, the monitoring system is open for whitewashing and manipulations.

At least among scholars, it is generally acknowledged that for example the change from a tribal society to the model of local autonomy is not only a technical or administrative issue but foremost a question of social change.[9] Following the Theory of Communicative Action of Jürgen Habermas[10] we can conceive social change as the result of a communication process among social actors, who are trying to push through their interests and world images, whereby the

---

[8] This has even been admitted by a GTZ-report looking on evaluation reports of decentralization projects in 14 different countries (GTZ - Stabstelle für Evaluierung, 2009).

[9] Talcott Parsons and Samuel N. Eisenstadt have addressed this problem of social change already very early and in a comprehensive way, cf. (Eisenstadt, 1973) .

[10] Habermas, 1984, cf. also Roschmann, 2003.

assertiveness of the actors involved plays an important role. If we use this concept to analyze the question, whether or not the essay of development programs to export Western-styled good governance concepts to tribal societies will be successful, the answer can be given in an easier way than established evaluation systems. The outcome of this analytical approach will depend on the factor, whether the Western concept will meet the needs of different actors in the society and therefore will find sufficient supporters. Only if the result of the analysis is "yes," the further question arises, whether or not it will be meaningful that donors provide technical and financial support to overcome the remaining hurdles. In contrast to the speculative tracing back of impact chains used in evaluation reports on development-aid programs, these facts are accessible to the instruments of social research. Therefore a feasible option to come to reliable results is not to find and verify causal chains between donor activities and observable events but to look on the likelihood that the stakeholder/actors of the respective society are willing and able to adopt Western concepts of good governance.

The following analysis is based on this approach and is looking at good governance projects in Cambodia, Indonesia and Cameroon, and it gives a brief overview of other projects in Africa, particularly in the area of decentralization. The results will show us that these donor activities are dammed to fail.

## III. Decentralization – a favored instrument of development cooperation

Decentralization, here understood as the delegation of central government functions to subnational or local units, has been promoted in the context of good governance approaches and became one of the most favored instruments of development cooperation. Decentralization programs have been launched in roughly one hundred countries in the world, even in the war-riddled South Sudan in 2013. The concept of decentralization seems to promise a solution to numerous problems. Corresponding development policies are perceived as being omnipotent, and are assumed to deliver considerable contributions in regard to poverty reduction and democratization.[11] To look at the impacts and outcomes of good governance programs, decentralization seems to be an appropriate and manageable field of research regarding the success of donor activities in this area. As donors point particularly to the poverty-reduction impact of decentralization programs, the question at the outset is: Is decentralization, as a *concept,* likely to reduce poverty, and can we therefore expect that decentralization will have at least in theory some positive effects on poverty alleviation?

It is safe to say that a more effective government system will lead to less poverty. Hence, the

---

[11] Steinich, 1997.

question then is: Is it likely that decentralization makes government systems more effective?

The list of reasons why decentralized government systems are an effective way to govern and administrate public affairs on the local or subnational level is long, [12] and the literature, pointing to these advantages fills the shelves of libraries. As a result of the insight that "all knowledge is local," the main argument is that decentralization will solve a lot management problems caused by information gaps of central governments. Decentralization is also believed to mitigate the principal-agent dilemma and to improve the transparency of decision-making processes. On the top the accountability of local governments will become significantly higher compared to central governments due to the proximity between local politicians and their electorate. Finally, it is usually much easier to activate private resources in favor of public affairs on the local level, not only from civil society organizations and individuals but also from private companies or the local elites. So there is strong evidence that decentralization in general can improve the effectiveness of the government system and in this way can contribute to poverty alleviation.

But of course this effect will only take place if citizens can substantially participate in the local decision-making process and feel they have a

---

[12] See Manor, 1997, for a representative view.

voice in local affairs. Therefore the delegation of functions to local branches of state agencies or the transfer of power to governors or district heads appointed by and accountable to the central government is not enough. Instead, a delegation of power to freely and fairly elected and largely independent local or subnational governments seems to be indispensable (so-called political/democratic decentralization) in order to benefit from the potential advantages of a decentralized government system.

However, having in place the political and legal framework for such a system is not only a necessary but an insufficient prerequisite for the success of decentralization reforms. The second and mostly neglected precondition is the characteristic of "portability" of concepts about social systems between different societies. In this context, the term portability refers to whether the decentralization-concept, which requires powerful, democratically elected and largely independent local governments, will work within in any society or not. The idea of local autonomy and municipal self-administration for example had taken root in Germany long before the famous *Preußische Städteordnung* (Prussian local government code) from November 19, 1808, and the reforms of Freiherr vom Stein had been practiced already hundreds of years before in largely independent medieval cities with municipal legislative, administrative and judiciary bodies.

Based on these long-time experiences, a coherent system with different government levels, shared competencies, fiscal-transfer and revenue-sharing mechanisms and sophisticated supervision functions was developed step-by-step. To run a system like this requires not only thousands of highly qualified administrators on all levels but also an army of engaged and well informed volunteer commune and district councils, devoting their leisure time to local politics. Needless to say, a complicated government system with hundreds or thousands of semi-autonomous entities needs a certain environment to function properly. The state-building process must be completed otherwise the rules for power and revenue sharing will not be respected. To avoid serious friction between stakeholders on different government levels, a certain understanding and tradition in regard to local autonomy is required. Therefore it is not enough that the quality and capacity of the government apparatus has reached already a very professional level. Stakeholders must be also feel bound to a culture of Max Weber's bureaucracy, where administrators and government officials are used to working neutrally and unselfishly in line with the law and in common interest. Last but not least, we need a high degree of civil society, a party system and free and independent media in order to interlink local governments and the individual citizen.

By contrast, in most developing countries the situation is quite different. The state-building process started only after independence and is not complete. Outside the capital, government functions remain in the hands of local strongmen, often operating in a legal limbo between traditional and state power. Albeit only a part of the power therefore is centralized and transferred to the state level, a tradition in regard to local administration doesn't exist. Instead of this, mostly *tribal/clan structures* still dominate, but they are not comparable to the model of municipal self-administration. Due to education problems the quality and capacity of the government apparatus, particularly on the local level, is low. Power of political leaders is mostly exerted not within the formal system stipulated by the law, but by the non-corporative structures of patron-client relations. What counts in the eyes of the population is the personal power of their leaders and not the formal competence a person is assumed to have according to an official position. The legal system therefore has only limited authority and the state bureaucracy isn't neutral. Instead the administrators are working in favor of their patron leaders. The idea of a civil society and party system is new to the population because authoritarian regimes have tried to quell their formation.

The gaps between Western societies and societies in developing countries in regard to precondition for a decentralized government system are evident. Hence, the question is: Is it possible to close this gap with the means of development cooperation or will at least the effects of evolution and globalization in the foreseeable future automatically lead to an assimilation of social orders in the "Third World?"

## IV. Theories of Modernization

For long time in Europe, history was understood as a single, coherent and evolutionary process. Karl Marx, whose concept of history and development was based on Hegel's mechanism of dialectic used words like "primitive" or "advanced," "traditional" or "modern," when referring to different types of human societies. The preface to the English edition of *Das Kapital* stated that *"The country that is more developed industrially only shows, to the less developed, the image of its own future."* For Hegel and Marx, there was a coherent development of human societies from simple tribes once based on slavery and subsistence agriculture, through various theocracies, monarchies, and feudal aristocracies, up through modern liberal democracy and technologically driven capitalism. This evolutionary process was neither random nor unintelligible, even if it did not proceed in a straight line, and even if it was not possible to question whether people were happier or better off as a result of historical "progress" when taking into account the experience of all peoples in all times. [13] This 19th century perception was still present when industrialized countries started

---

[13] Fukuyama, 1992, S. 68.

19

their development aid projects in the aftermath of the Second World War. Probably the most influential among these theories was Walt Whitman Rostow's theory about the five stages of economic growth,[14] published in 1960. Similar to Marx, he postulated that economic growth occurs in five basic stages: traditional society, preconditions for take-off, take-off, drive to maturity, and age of high mass consumption. The last stage characterized modern Western societies, where the "take-off," marked by urbanization, industrialization proceeds and technological breakthroughs, occurred in the 19th century and took about 20 years (vanguard Great Britain: 1783-1802). This perception of development as a unilinear evolution process from "traditional" to "modern" societies made development bureaucrats believe that programs on financial and technical aid can speed up the developing process and the problems can be fixed with the same "toolbox kits" in all developing countries.

Even this view was criticized early on for its "euro-centrism" by several scientists. The real turnaround occurred only since the beginning of the 1990s. On one hand then the understanding had grown that development is not only about economics and that reality is much more complex as all models of stages could explain. The recognition prevailed increasingly that different

---

[14] Rostow, 1960.

ways of development are possible and that we cannot assume that developing countries follow the same path Western countries have taken in the past. The general conclusion from this is: We cannot simply rebuild Western societies in developing countries.

Nowadays scientific approaches don't try to deliver an encompassing theory of development anymore, but like transformation theories they attempt to explain certain mechanisms mostly on the base of the theory of action, going back to Max Weber. From this point of view it is more important to try to predict what stakeholders are going to do in the particular situation of their country than to explain the tide of history. Following this approach the basic assumption is that decentralization reforms and other Western concepts like democracy, rule of law, etc. will only be successful in developing counties if stakeholders in these countries feel attracted to the underlying ideas. This raises the question of whether the fact that these concepts have proven to make the government system more effective and therefore promise to improve public welfare is sufficient to convince stakeholders in developing countries to undertake huge social chances. But before we turn to the problem of indicators and criteria for their willingness to put this kind of reform project on the agenda, we have to answer the question of whether or not it is possible at all to predict their further behavior and actions.

If we believe in the concept of free will, whereby individuals are free and can do whatever they like, human behavior is principally incalculable. However it is obvious that driving forces, which philosophers since Plato have called "desire" and "reason," are pushing men in a certain direction and make their decisions in a certain way predictable.[15] In addition a mixture of economic interests, empirical knowledge, virtue, values, historic background, culture, religion and mutual expectations forms institutions, or, as Douglas North has called them, the rules of the game. Taken as a whole, these institutions make up the social order of the society. This social order is more or less the "stakeholder corridor" that channels the free will and the actions of human beings.[16]

The precise knowledge about the factors shaping this stakeholder corridor makes human behavior even more foreseeable. If we go back to the aforementioned theory of communicative action of Jürgen Habermas, social change is the permanent discourse among social actors about alteration of the mentioned institution according to their interests and world images. As individuals usually belong to social groups and layers of society we can assemble individuals in groups of stakeholders with similar perceptions and interests and map out conflict lines and

---

[15] See figure 1
[16] North, 1990.

coalition opportunities among these groups. This and an estimation of the collective resources of the different groups will tell us how likely it is, for example, for good governance reforms which try to replace a patron-client system by bureaucracy, to succeed.

**Figure 1 The Stakeholder corridor**

As we have already seen, in most of the developing countries corrupt and rent-seeking elites are dominating not only the government and the security forces but also an important part of the economy. The other part of society is shaped by a poor and largely badly educated population. A significant middle class doesn't exist. Under these preconditions we can assume that even though good governance reforms would make the government system much more effective neither the elites/government nor the government apparatus will support such projects because this runs not only counter to their main interests but poses a serious threat to their physical existence. In most of these countries corruption, embezzlement, and the violation of basic human right are crimes under the existing law, and the members of current elites would probably be the first who would be taken to the court if they would allow an independent judiciary and powerful legislative bodies. The population is unfamiliar with ideas like democracy, accountability, power sharing, decentralization, etc. and too weak to form civil society organizations with roots in society, independent from external supports.

Even international donors (foreign governments and international organizations) should not act as stakeholders in the light of the principle of state sovereignty. By means of development aid, they try to shape society in developing countries, but due to their lack of knowledge about the complex political, social, cultural and religious background of the societies in these countries, this way of support remains mostly inappropriate. Moreover, if we compare the billions of EUR and the army of specialists dedicated to turning East Germany - similar to Cambodia in population and size - into a liberal democracy after the Berlin Wall came down with the means available to cope with the much bigger challenges in developing countries, the insignificance of the donor activities becomes obvious. After all, there seems to be strong evidence that donor programs are doomed to fail.

## V. Cambodia - Decentralization reforms à la Hun Sen

### 1. The Stakeholder – Corridor

The Khmer Empire was founded in 802 AD by Jayavarman II, who declared himself king. During a period of 600 years it dominated much of Southeast Asia. After a decay of power, Cambodia was ruled in the following centuries as a vassal between its neighbors. In 1863 it became a protectorate of France, and gained independence in 1953 under King Sihanouk. As a side event of the Vietnam War in Cambodia, the Khmer Rouge under Pol Pot came to power and maintained a terror regime between 1975 and 1979 before getting ousted by Vietnam's army and the Vietnamese backed People's Republic of Kampuchea forces. The Khmer Rouge had totally destroyed the old social order in order to erect their "stone-age style" society. After one decade of socialistic rule during the occupation by Vietnam, Cambodia was governed briefly by a United Nations mission (1992-1993). Thereafter it became finally a constitutional kingdom based on a constitution, promising the people democracy and the rule of law. However the new Kingdom was a democracy without democrats. Prime Minister Hun Sen at the helm of the Cambodian People's Party (CPP) has remained the leading power since 1985 under different political orders and he has governed the country in a semi-authoritarian way. The opposition was formed by royalists, not really renowned for their democratic conviction. Similar to other democratization experiments the main hurdle was and remains that only the elites have access to collective resources and the power to claim land. The bulk of the badly educated and poor population is used to living in patron-client relationships in the countryside. Government services are low and the corruption rate is one of the highest in the world, and practically nobody, on the side of the population as well as on the side of the government, had had any experience with local autonomy or in public participation when the decentralization reform process started in 2001.

Albeit the state-building process was mostly complete at this time, modern law had not penetrated society. Even today the recognition of the new legal system is still low and in most cases the maxim "might makes right" applies in daily life. Recent surveys and interviews indicate that the population conceives the government as leadership but not as the representative of the citizenry. [17] Private matters are not separated from public affairs and political leaders exert their power through a network of personal relationships and not by the competence provided by their public office. These patron-client relations are the backbone of society and up to now most of the people don't identify themselves as "citizens." But by destroying the old order the

---

[17] Becker, 2014.

Khmer Rouge also destroyed the traditional limitations of the power of patrons. The new CPP patrons, who have replaced the aristocratic system by the mechanisms of neo-patrimonialism (but who are significantly still called *Oknya* in Khmer language), therefore can act largely without social restrictions. Moreover this, the political regime under Hun Sen is distinctly non-corporatist. Hun Sen may have pursued a corporatist strategy to the extent that he promoted an organic ideology of national unity and attempted to direct political mobilization along controlled channels. But he is rarely using bureaucratic formulas of influence to conduct authoritative institutions or to grant a certain amount of influence to interest groups within civil society.

Land grabbing and eviction have become the most pressing problems, not only for peasants in the countryside. Also people living on their land already for decades can easily become victims to shopping mall and office tower projects of powerful tycoons when their parcels get in range of the steadily growing city centers.

In sum, we have to conclude that the current borderlines of the stakeholder corridor are not likely to channel the actions of Cambodian political actors in direction of democracy, rule of the law or the idea of Western-styled local autonomy. But this situation is not carved in stone of course and may change if powerful interest groups within the society become more and more convinced that a system of good governance and a higher degree of local autonomy is more in their favor than the existing neo-patrimonial framework. Such a change in the mindset could be triggered for example if parts of society start to doubt the legitimacy of the Hun Sen Regime or, at least theoretically, if donor-driven awareness-raising and empowerment campaigns show their results.

## 2. The stakeholders

The term of "stakeholder" stands here for a formal or informal group of actors who close ranks for pursuing common interests. In context of the decentralization reform process in Cambodia we can identify four main stakeholders.

a. The most important stakeholder is made up of the elites. Cambodian elites are composed of the CPP leaders who are at the same time men at the helm of the Royal Cambodian Government. Even when there are internal disputes and different party wings pursuing different agendas the common interest to remain in power and to defend their economic dominance keeps them firmly together and fences them off from other social groups.

b. The government apparatus, particularly the government official in the various ministries, forms the second stakeholder due to its personal relationships and its *esprit de corps*.

c. The population, here understood as the part of society who belongs neither to the elites nor to the government apparatus, usually consists of different stakeholders. However, Cambodian society is not divided in easily identifiable groups of actors, as formal cooperation is rare or, if visible, only reflects a facade but not the real structure of cooperation and subordination. Therefore it is subject to further analyses to look into the question of which stakeholders we can identify in the population, if any.

d. Difficult to classify is also the role of international donors and donor organizations. Formally they pretend only to act as supporters of reform processes where only their Cambodian counterparts have a stake. It is true that the election of local leaders in 2001 was initiated by the RCG without direct external pressure. But we will see forthwith that this reform has had initially a totally different intention than donors have thought and the enthusiasm of donors, who believed that the Hun Sen regime was going to start a democratization process and tried to get the population via participation into the boat, was simply a misinterpretation. Due to the fact that a proper and coherent legal terminology doesn't exist in Khmer, the translation of legal documents is more than difficult. Khmer words like (in English transcription) *khum, phum* and *nité bokul* etc., are usually translated to commune, village and legal entity. These translations are not really correct as these terms have a different connotation for

Westerners. The resulting misperception on the side of donor organizations is preventing them from understanding that the Cambodian reforms are far away from the Western-style model of decentralization. Therefore the international donor community is trying to support a reform project that the RCG never launched, and instead has its own different agenda. However due to their financial resources, the Western backers of decentralization are sitting mostly in the driver seat of the "formal" reform process, and in this way, the "community" of donors has to be perceived as stakeholder, too. This causes the problem that donors are forming an "external" stakeholder, acting from outside of the stakeholder corridor which applies to Cambodian actors.

## 3. Will Cambodian stakeholders adopt the idea of decentralization?

### a) Elites and the ruling party

As mentioned, the elites who recruit their members from the upper level of CPP leaders and who represent at the same time the top leaders of the different government branches are mostly former Khmer Rouge cadres and wartime enemies of many opposition leaders. As Markus Karbaum[18] has argued in his book "Cambodia under Hun Sen," deep ingrained distrust

---

[18] Karbaum, 2008

characterizes the relations among politicians of the ruling party and the opposition. Every concession in regard to power is interpreted as a sign of weakness, and as power is directly linked with the access to collective resources, to share power means to share resources with the enemy. But the lack of social trust[19] is not only a problem between CPP and opposition parties or organizations of civil society not under control of the CPP. There is also a lack of democratic behavior and habits inside of political parties and other organizations, because strong hierarchical structures are prevailing. The elites have been fighting for their position of power and their current economic welfare in a dangerous struggle for more than 20 years. In a certain way it is understandable that most of them now feel it is time to enjoy the fruits of those harsh times. An intention to transfer power to institutions that are not 100 percent under the control of the CPP leadership is not visible among the elites. The more successful the opposition parties are (like the newly founded Cambodia National Rescue Party [CNRP] [20] , which even under unfair conditions won 55 out of 123 seats in the National Assembly in the elections in 2013), the stronger the CPP's grip on political power will become, too.

---

[19] Bratton has named the trust among the different actor "social capital" (Bratton, 1994, p.3)
[20] CNSP is a merger from the former Sam Rainsy Party and Human Rights Part. But seemingly the only common goal these both former parties has united them is to win the next elections against CPP.

This is why CPP leaders never had the intention to share power or to give people the chance to participate in a significant way in decision-making processes, when they introduced the local election law and the law on the administration of communes and sangkats[21] in the year 2000, the base for the first election of commune and sangkat councilors in the current Cambodia. Instead the decentralization reform served three other purposes from the beginning. Firstly, it was an instrument to penetrate the state territory by CPP structures, even in the most rural countryside. CPP commune councilors were therefore simply representatives on the spot who have to execute the instructions of the leaders in the capital in a more subtle way. On top this model has also had the advantage of channeling local-level donor funds in a direction which is in line with interests of CPP headquarters. The second reason was that CPP had lost support in the population due to the unacceptable behavior of some of its local leaders. The elections therefore were a smart way to resolve this problem. Thirdly, the Hun Sen government was still under fire at this time for its *coup d'etat* in 1997, and the announcement of local elections had calmed down donor critics without substantial changes which could compromise the general political direction of the government.

---

[21] *Sangkat* is the city-district in the bigger cities which don't belong to a state-district (*srok*).

CPP elites are dominating all government branches and huge parts of the economy and the media up to a level we can already call "state capture." As a result of all this it seems to be safe to say that the CPP elites are the most powerful players in Cambodian society but also the most powerful opponent to Western-style ideas like decentralization reforms.

### b) Government apparatus

The administrative substructure of the RCG, hereinafter referred to as government apparatus, has an important role in implementing politics and therefore is principally under the control of the government. But as mentioned, Cambodian leaders are used to rule in an incorporative way. For example, the Governor of Svay Rieng Province and former Commissioner of the National Police, Hok Lundy, who is formally subordinate to the Minister of Interior Sar Kheng, can probably decide very independently from his superior due to the fact that he is the brother-in-law to the premier minister. The government apparatus therefore often has a life of its own. Corresponding to the model of neo-patrimonialism the government apparatus consists of various competing patron-client networks. These networks are often built around the formal structure of the state bureaucracy and often we will find numerous members of the same family working on different positions in the same state agency, tied to one person whom they call mostly the "*oknay*."[22] To safeguard and protect the position of the *oknay*, on whom their own position and the position of the other family member depends, is the overall goal. This creates not only the already mentioned "*esprit de corps*" among the rank and file of a government entity but makes the staff also solely accountable to their patrons and not to the population. Due to the fact that the official salary for civil servants is far away from the amount required to make a living, for most of the government officials corruption and embezzlement is practically unavoidable in order to survive. As a consequence, positions and power which allow generation of these kinds of revenues are handed down from the patron to his clients in exchange for money. It is obvious and frequently confirmed by government officials in private discussions that it is almost impossible to work for the government and not be corrupt.[23] Reforms like decentralization, which intend to make the government system more transparent and public servants accountable to the people, are compromising the existing system and are therefore not welcome.

In regard to anti-corruption, initiatives of donor's government agency usually pursue a very

---

[22] In former times this was a general designation of high-ranking government officials, usually coming from aristocratic families (Chandler, 2008)
[23] See also Luco, 2003.

34

successful strategy which has stood the test of time already for more than 20 years. Toward donors everybody shows enthusiasm and good will to reform, listens to advisors at various donor workshops and conferences (as long as a good location and sufficient per diem are provided), and fine policy papers drafted by Western advisors are ceremonially adopted. However, during the subsequent implementation process the reforms get scattered to the four winds in subtle ways.

Here, too, we have to conclude that the government apparatus is a powerful player but not at all a supporter of the decentralization reform.

### c) Population[24]

For the very most part of Cambodian history the government never has provided public services or something comparable. If people have been confronted with the government it was only for the purpose of forced labor or tax collection. Even after independence in 1953, which came along with a liberal constitution, democracy and a touch of the rule of law, the idea of civil society remained unknown. This applies also to the concept of citizenship, which is already demonstrated by the fact that a word, which could express this idea, doesn't exist in Khmer

---

[24] The word "society" is intentionally not used in this context, because for most of the Cambodians still this concept doesn't really exist in their perception.

language. The Khmer word that is used instead (in transcription to English: *"pol rot"*[25]) has much more a connotation of the term "subject," and indeed, most of the population is still living personally subordinated in local patron-client networks. Sustaining this dominate collective experience which has shaped Cambodians is the fact that political clashes only end up in war, violence and much more misery. Former King Sihanouk is cited to have said in 1954 to French diplomats: *"[...] [T]hose following democracy in Cambodia are either bourgeois or princes. [...] The Cambodian people are children. They know nothing about politics. And they care less."*[26] In a certain way this seems to be still true today. Surveys are showing that ordinary Cambodians mostly not have even a basic understanding of the government system.[27] Though they welcome the right to elect the government, this is not linked to any political programs or policies. In the perception of most of the Cambodians the members of the government represent their leaders and they expect that they act as leaders. Seemingly people usually aim to have "good" leaders who take care of their needs and improve their welfare. But to find ways to fulfill these wishes, in their opinion, is exactly the job of the leaders and not of the people.

---

[25] "Pol" means something like army or allegiance and "rot" means the people.
[26] Quoted from Chandler, 2008, p. 72.
[27] Becker, 2014, p. 341 f..

Of course in the meantime also in Cambodia a very thin layer of middle class people has emerged. These middle class people are more aware of the political system and off the records they are criticizing the Hun Sen regime. But most of them also belong to the circle of beneficiaries and openly opposing the political system is therefore no option.

As the poor performance of CPP during the last elections to the National Assembly demonstrates, the bulk of lower class people is obviously extremely discontented with the government due to numerous cases of land grabbing and the low minimum wages. But besides some massive demonstrations of protest in the capitol caused by suspicions of electoral fraud in the aftermath of the 2013 elections, most people are remaining inactive. As a result we have to conclude that even among the population the number of people supporting concepts like democracy and decentralization is very low.

### d) Civil Society

Seanglim Bit has written in 1991: *"It is noteworthy that Cambodian Culture has not developed any other social institutions or groups beyond the family structure which might facilitate the concept of collective social responsibility. Cambodia does not have a tradition of associations, volunteer groups, trade unions, or other network composed of people who come together for a common purpose.[...] Opportunities for exchanging experience, cooperation, or identifying with a larger group are restricted to groups which already forms the basis for a social identity, namely family and village."* [28] Hence, when donor organizations arrived in Cambodia in the 1990s with their funds for democratizing Cambodia, they were desperately looking for partners on the level of civil society. However, to enthuse somebody for this idea in a country where the idea of "society" was still an unknown concept and people don't call themselves citizens, proved to be very difficult. But at the same time Cambodians, who have made it to escape the Khmer Rouge regime and have found asylum for decades in France or the United States, started to return to Cambodia. These people, many of them grown up and educated abroad and therefore speaking the language of the Western donors perfectly, have become the ideal cooperation partners in regard to democratization programs albeit most of them have become strangers in their own country. As money didn't play a serious role, within a couple of years NGOs started to mushroom at every corner, soon reaching the number of close to 3,000 organizations. Even though these NGO's clearly haven't grown out of Cambodian society but have been created and are maintained only by foreign funds, donors don't get tired calling them the "civil society." It is undeniable that some of these organizations like the Cambodian League for the

---

[28] Bit, 1991

Promotion and Defense of Human Rights (LICADHO) are doing a really good job in favor of the people. But most of them are outsiders to the Cambodian society and only a tool for donors to spend their money for workshops or awareness-raising campaigns with doubtable outcomes.

On the other hand the names of the leaders of national organizations in the sector of charity, sports or youth organizations read like the "who's who" in Cambodia's high society. Bun Rany Hun Sen, the wife of the Prime minister for example, acts since 1998 as President of the Cambodia Red Cross. Even the helm of the National Association of Cambodian Scouts (NACS) is occupied by a high-ranking CPP leader, Deputy Prime Minister Sok An.

Hence, if we talk about civil society in Cambodia we have to keep in mind that this has less to do with civil society in Western countries. Most of the donor supported NGOs may promote the idea of decentralization. But because of their lack of roots into the Cambodian society, their stance has no real significance in the perception of Cambodian people. The other part of NGOs is dominated by the elites and therefore not open to these kind of ideas.

Hence, our analysis leads to the conclusion that there is no stakeholder in Cambodia society who is willing and able to push the reforms ahead, but with the elites and the government apparatus there are powerful opponents to the concept.

## e) International Donor

As we have seen at the outset international donors still believe seemingly in outdated theories of modernization. As a consequence their focus rests on technical details like capacity building and awareness raising even though the problem is obviously in the first line not the gap of knowledge but the discrepancy in regard to social values and overall concepts which of course cannot be changed by workshops and conferences. Neither the RCG under Hun Sen nor the population will change their mindsets only because some Western advisors don't get tired of explaining to them that democracy, rule of law and centralization is good, and corruption, nepotism and embezzlement of public funds is bad for the country.[29]

Besides this general failure of their development cooperation approach, donors permanently have to cope with their own administrative problems. This is mainly caused by the fact that they have to spend their money by Western standards of administration in a country where totally different rules apply. The main part of donor organizations depends on revenues from overhead costs which they receive from their backers in form of a certain percentage of the funds they are commissioned to manage. Hence, spending the entire budget provided for their program within a clearly defined time frame becomes mostly more

---

[29] Similar: Fukuyama, 2004, p. 87.

important than the effectiveness of the program itself.

In addition, even though donor organizations of course assert, their staff is selected from a pool of international experts, the human resource problem is undeniable. Among the more than 500 foreign advisors is not one handful of persons mastering the Khmer language and most of them are unfamiliar with the details of Cambodian culture or the problems of people living in the countryside. In regard to professional skills we will hardly find somebody among the decentralization specialists who have already worked in this sector at home or have purchased experience with government systems from outside of developing countries.

Joel Brinkley has in his article "Aid to Cambodia rarely reaches the people it's meant to help"[30] also pointed to the self-interest of international staff of donor-organizations to stay in a city like Phnom Penh which "*is a relatively pleasant place to live. Rents are cheap and household help is even cheaper. Espresso bars and stylish restaurants dot the river front — primarily for diplomats and aid workers.*" This may explain why nobody working for donor organizations likes to report home that his program is unsuccessful due to the resistance of his partners in the Cambodia government. It's more likely that he will report home the reforms will take more time

---

[30] Brinkley, 2011.

to be implemented and therefore he will suggest to extend the program for another three years or so. Of course donors frequently have evaluation programs in place in order to measure the success of their programs. But most of these programs are not more than window dressing. As already demonstrated, the movements in a society are much too complex to be measured by a couple of program indicators and judged by a review based on a brief visit by an evaluator.

## 4. Conclusion

In the case of Cambodia it is obvious that good governance programs like the support to decentralization reform will not be successful or provide benefits for poor Cambodians as the concepts don't find the support of any powerful interest group inside of Cambodian society. The elites and their entourages in the government are natural opponents of every reform that leads to power sharing, more transparency of decision-making processes or public control. The so-called civil society is mostly made up be donor-funded organizations that are not interlinked with the population and therefore cannot trigger changes in the mindset. Moreover, the main donor activities like capacity building activities, technical advice in legal drafting issues and policy paper development operate at the totally wrong level of development and therefore fulminate without any significant impact.

## VI. Cameroon – Tribal society instead of local autonomy

The present political situation is similar to Cambodia. In regard to the size of the population and the territory as well as to the geographical location, Cameroon is comparable to Cambodia. After the World War I and the defeat of the German colonial power most of today's Cameroon came as a League of Nations mandate under French rule. A smaller part was administered by the British. In 1961 the French territory gained independence and merged successively with the British part which became independent, too. But in contrast to the Angkor Empire in Cambodia, Cameroon was composed of a patchwork of more the 250 fairly small tribal territories with local kings and chiefs, and the colonial powers have been interested only in the country's resources - not in governing its citizens with a national identity. Hence, the perception to be "Cameroonian" didn't cross the mind of the people living on the territory. Western colonial power decided to call it Cameroon.

The main task of those who gain power after independence was to build a state and to form a nation out of tribal men living more or less by chance within this territory and suddenly should became one people. Besides the personal desire to stay in power this was the main reason why Ahmadou Ahidjo, first prime minister and later president of Cameroon, established very soon an authoritarian dictatorship based on a one-party system with the support of his French backers.[31] Even the initial constitution was democratic and liberal, Ahidjo's party, the R.D.P.C. (*Rassemblement démocratique du Peuple Camerounais,* People's Democratic Movement) and its sub-organizations became the single political force to be officially accepted. His successor, the French educated lawyer Paul Biya, initially tried to modernize Cameroon's society, but pulled back after a coup d'état against him was launched. Under the rule of Ahidjo, the state-building process has been fostered by creating an increasing number of positions in the government for local strongmen in order to integrate them into the system and make them become R.D.P.C. followers. But when the financial crises in the 1980s hit Cameroon too, [32] the huge number of government officials on the country's payroll imposed an unbearable burden to the debt-riddled state budget and forced the state to reduce the costs of the state government apparatus. The ousted part of the elites, who lost their privileges due to these austerity programs, started to form a standby opposition and asserted to fight for the liberty of the people. Francoise Mitterrand, the French President, finally convinced Paul Biya in 1992 to reintroduce a multi-party system and allow free elections. Particularly in the English-speaking Northwest

---

[31] Mehler, 2008, p. 40
[32] The debts of Cameroon increased between 1982 and 1992 from US$ 2.8 billion to US$ 7.4 billion.

region, the SDF with Fru Ndi, a local aristocrat and former R.D.P.C. minister, at the helm, gained support. He ran for President but failed to win with 35 percent of the votes, in a tight race obviously influenced by electoral fraud of the Biya administration. With 38 percent, Biya was declared the winner and remained in office. However, due to a similar tight outcome of the election to the National Assembly and public protests against Biyas regime, he was forced to share power with the opposition leaders. In 1996, a new constitution was promulgated, promising to transfer power to the regional and the local level. A second chamber, the Senate, as a representation body of the regions, was set to be created. The assignment to introduce mechanisms of decentralization became a legal obligation for the government in Yaoundé. Finally, the number of terms to be re-elected as state president was limited to a maximum of one.

But in reality things developed quite differently from that. To start with the last amendment: The tenure-limit for the office of the president was abolished in 2010 and Biya became president once again. The constitutional obligation to introduce the Senate was fulfilled after 17 years in 2013 and is probably part of a package to determine the political heritage of Paul Biya.

In regard to promised decentralization, Western donors have been quickly on the spot with their support to democratization and local development programs. But it was not before 2004 that any legislation on the role of local governments has been enacted. Like in the case of Cambodia, the large volume of the legal texts didn't automatically mean a plus of power for the municipalities. The competence of mayors and local councils remains fairly unclear and the degree of state-tutelage high and comprehensive. Like in Cambodia council membership depends on party memberships. As a consequence council members, far away from being representatives of the local population, are only marionettes of the politician in the headquarters of the political parties.

The transfer of financial resources over which local governments can decide independently remained also close to zero, and for most of public services central government agencies *(Service déconcentre étatique, SDE)* are in charge. Even though since 2010 the annual state budget provides at first glance a considerable amount of money for investments on the local level, most of this money is spent for feasibility studies or similar activities by the sector ministries and vanishes then in one way or the other via consultant contracts etc. This is the reason why the funds which finally arrive at the local level are mostly insufficient to realize the intended project (for example: construction of a school building) physically. If the available budget really allows the local government to start the construction work, the mayor or the commune councilors don't have any discretion at all during the realization process but are obligated to follow precise instruction of the sector ministries.

In the past the budget of the sector ministries have been treated like the private funds of their ministers who could spend the money arbitrarily and haven't been accountable towards someone other than their patron, the President Paul Biya. Based on the Paris Declaration on Aid Effectiveness, signed in 2005, donors however insisted on adapting the management of public finances and expenditures to Western standards. As this grievance was typical for most of the African countries, the donor community with the World Bank at the front developed the so-called *"Chaine P.P.B.S (planification-programmation-budgétisation-suivi)."* This term stands for a comprehensive and integrative top-down planning tool with clear stipulated mechanism for every stage of the management process of government funds. At least in theory this approach seems to be suitable to fighting against the waste of public funds - but only in theory. The first critical point of this instrument is that even in highly industrialized Western countries a state planning system like the *"Chaine P.P.B.S."* is rarely found for good reasons. At the base of this chain is namely the "Cameroon Vision 2035," a national strategy intended to guide the country's development for the next 30 years. Besides skepticism whether the development goals are achievable,[33] the question is, whether an overall

---

[33] Tata, 06. February 2013)

30-year strategy really makes sense. If past experience is indicative, this strategy will be outdated soon due to the unpredictable course of history. The strategy naturally is restricted to very general goals and statements which cannot give direct operation instructions. The strategy was then translated into the *"Stratégie pour la croissance et l'emploi,"* a 10-year strategy paper aiming to support economic growth and employment on the same high level of abstraction. Because neither politicians nor the state bureaucracy is interested and capable of condensing it down to its practical application based in the real world. So even if the essence of the strategy is common ground, nobody has an idea about the meaning of all these documents.

By the tools of *Chain P.P.B.S.* local governments are now expected to have elaborate five-year development plans which are in line with the overreaching national strategies. As in most African countries, in Cameroon decisions are usually made on a daily basis and due to occasional events but not as part of planning processes or a vision for the next five years. To draft development plans therefore seems to be suspect in the eyes of local politicians. Donors therefore provide support programs for the elaboration of the planning documents by external advisors. Even the consultation and participation of the public is foreseen; the public hearings remain mostly a farce without substantial input of the local population. Due to time and budget limits, at the end the external advisor feels forced to satisfy donor expectations by producing a complicated development plan, encompassing several hundred pages and dozens of tables and graphics, but meaningless to the mayor and the commune councils. After copies of the development plan have been submitted to the planning bureaucracy of the different ministries, it vanishes in a drawer in the mayor's office and local governments go ahead with their decision-making processes as they have always done before.

On the next stage it is the task of the Ministry for Economy and National Planning to compile these documents, produced for the more than 250 municipalities in Cameroon, in order to develop in coordination with the sector ministries sector agendas and to provide the required budget. Due to the fact that communal development plans don't follow a uniform schema and guiding parameters are missing, making the submitted data comparable and matching with planning parameters applying on the national level is practically impossible. Besides the factor that the outcome of the planning process is mostly not the result of a rational decision-making process but of neo-patrimonial networking practices and clientelism, the funds granted for communal projects have rarely something to do with the initial local development plans. Hence, even if the local government would have put in the hours to produce a rational local five-year development agenda, the realization chances are more than low. At the end the donor-promoted planning system does not only increase bureaucracy and tend to waste government capacity needed urgently otherwise, but it also impedes the donor goal to foster local autonomy.

This becomes even more visible when we are looking at donor-funded decentralization programs. One of the focuses is the support of civil society. As in Cambodia, civil society in a Western sense of the word doesn't exist in Cameroon, and most of the civil society organizations *(Organisations société civil, OSC)* are therefore created only as a result of donor subsidies.[34] In order to improve public services of municipalities, activities are launched by aiding the OSC for public budget planning. This is done regardless of the fact that almost all of the relevant investments depend on central government funds out of the reach of mayors or commune councilors. Hence, workshops and public hearings are staged, mostly producing not much more than an unrealistic "shopping-list." On the top, mayors can agree easily to this kind of planning as the nomenclature for local budgets and annual accountability records doesn't provide a formula which makes visible whether the projects have been included in the annual budget or not. The annual budget that is available in reality to commune councils is on average about US$1 – US$3 per capita. This is an amount which is easily surpassed by the costs for workshops,

---

[34] Becker/Kopp, 2014, p. 89.

public hearings and consulting work conducted by OSEs and funded by donors. As soon as donors stop financing this process communes will not be able to bear the cost of a *"budget participative"* any more, even in the unlikely case that they feel this is a helpful administrative tool. Behind the science local budget planning is made in a traditional way, free of cost (and probably more effective), namely by agreements between the mayor, the traditional chief and village head men. So if donors would not try to install their own Western perception of decentralization but listen to grass roots people and foster their existing models of local autonomy, local governments would be better off in regard to budget issues.

This conclusion doesn't apply only for budget issues but to the whole decentralization process. As mentioned before, when Cameroon gained independence it had been a patchwork of tribal areas but no state. Since then the government in the capital has centralized state-power to a certain degree but state-authority has never fully penetrated into the countryside. Outside of the two metropolises Yaoundé und Douala, the traditional social order with local kings and chiefs, clans and the *"grandes familles"* is still dominant, because it is an important factor in context of the daily survival of most of the people living in remote areas. There is no court, no police, no land nor civil registry office etc. within reach for most of the inhabitants and the costs of official procedures and documents are unbearable. Hence in case of quarrels about property rights, the grassland or the heritage, for the marriage procedure, the birth certificate, the traditional chiefs are still the only existing resource of authority.

The same applies for basic public services like water supply, the education system, health insurance or bank services, rarely available to many people or only in exchange for high under-table payments. Local "*tontines*" and "*mutuelles,*" informal, small associations among people with close personal relationships like neighbors, villagers, or colleagues at work running a pump station, borrow money to pay the school fee or the doctor invoice. These few examples show the existence of a well-organized "civil society" in Cameroon, but, of course, this kind of civil society has nothing to do with the concept brought into being by Western thinkers like Hegel, Alexis de Tocqueville or Karl Marx. Like in Cambodia, associations or institutions among people who are not tied together by family or tribal relation and based on a certain degree of hierarchy are not common to the society in Cameroon.

As a consequence autochthony based on tribal-identity is very present in the daily life. Even the offspring of migrant laborers mostly feel only affiliated with their village of origin; they are often not accepted as equal "citizens" at the place where they are living; and they are excluded from local decision making processes. "*People should cast their ballots where they wish to be buried*" is one of the popular proposals deriving from the fact that the corps of descendants are still brought back to the villages where their family initially comes from. Moreover this clanship is not only a local issue but plays also a decisive role in national politics. The clan of the Betis, to whom Paul Biya and most of his entourage belong, has been very successful in preventing members of the competing business-minded Bameliki from entering politics, even at the expense of national economic growth.

All this proves that governance in Cameroon is still much more a question of personal affiliations than of ruling over a certain territory. This runs, of course, counter to the idea of the principle of a modern territorial state that lies at the heart of Western good governance concepts like decentralization.

As a result in reality most of Cameroonians rely more on the traditional institutions than on local government. While mayors or councilors are mostly conceived as corrupt and unreliable representatives of the government in Yaoundé who prefer to spend most of their time in the capital, traditional chiefs, bound to the rules of customs and habits, are still the source of safety and warmth.

Development bureaucrats, particularly when based in donor headquarters in Washington, Bonn or Eschborn, seemingly are unaware of the reality on the ground. The source for their information about Cameroon is obviously events in five-star hotels where they meet with government officials, trained at French universities who are the main beneficiaries of Western funds. International staff, living in nice houses in Yaoundé's embassy district of Bastos often married with Cameroonians or having kids at school don't have any reasons to create doubts about the effectiveness of their programs. Local staff is mostly aware of the gap between donor ideas and the reality in the society, but their employers never ask for their honest opinion. They cannot risk their well-paid jobs and, moreover, they never would dare to criticize their white masters. Hence, instead of paving the way for improvement of the traditional system of "local autonomy," Western decentralization programs stick to their old ideas[35] and attempt to turn around the whole social order — a mission impossible, of course. Therefore, like in the case of Cambodia, donor aid in Cameroon, at best, will remain meaningless. More likely is that good governance programs hamper further development as they tie resources urgently required at other places to projects without sustainability.

## VII. Indonesia - *Autonomi Khusus* in Aceh and the windfall winners

In Indonesia good governance projects got a push

---

[35] Typically the World Bank report. „Cameroon - The Path to Fiscal Decentralization. Opportunities and Challenges (World Bank, 2012).

after the Asian economic crisis of 1997 hit Indonesia. Violent protests forced Haji Mohamed Suharto, in office as president with Western support since 1967, finally to step down on May 21, 1998. This was also the end to one of the most centralistic regimes in the world. Under his successor, B. J. Habibie, who studied and lived in Germany from 1955–1974, the new Indonesia Parliament attempted to introduce a more liberal and democratic political system. To assure that an authoritarian regime will not return, power was transferred in a so call "Big Bang" decentralization reform process in a comprehensive way to provincial and local governments. This was a risky project in a county counting about 240 million inhabitants with dozens of different languages and cultures, living on more the 12,000 islands.

Most problematic above all was the situation in Aceh, a province at the north tip of Sumatra, where the GAM[36] rebel group had been fighting for independence for more than 30 years. The political situation was very tense when on December 26, 2004 the waves of the deadliest tsunami in history ripped through Aceh, killing 221,000 people and leaving more than 500,000 displaced. The disaster paved the way to the Helsinki Peace accord between the rebels and the central government in Jakarta and led to a special autonomy *(autonomi khusus)* for the

---

[36] *Gerakan Aceh Merdeka* (Aceh Liberation Movement).

strongly Muslim-affiliated province. In order to help the victims, hundreds of millions of donor funds swamped the area, not only for reconstruction work but also to support the new semi-autonomous provincial and local governments. Hence, donors didn't only build new houses, streets, hospitals, health-centers, schools, centers for vocational training etc., but they also tried to improve the legal framework for the health system, the financial management and the spatial planning system, to introduce a population administration, to provide access to justice and so on. For this purpose training centers have been set up. Countless workshops and conferences for government officials, doctors, teachers and administrators have been held in expensive hotels. Airlines had to extend their services dramatically due to the stream of foreign advisors and public servants, now frequently commuting between Jakarta and Banda Aceh. With donor funds a huge airport was constructed, anticipating long-haul aircrafts arriving soon directly from Europe or the United States. In 2005 about US$ 2 billion have been available to *Badan Rehabilitasi dan Rekonstruksi (BRR)*, the state authority in charge for the coordination of the funds for reconstruction.

But even the physical realization of the most of the project failed. For example, much money was invested to produce legal documents and install government bodies in order to create a maritime hub, which was intended to become a competitor of Singapore. Like the highway thought to link

Banda Aceh with Medan (an economic hub at the Sumatra Street), a geothermal power plant foreseen to be financed by German KfW and many other projects never became reality. Most symbolic perhaps is the fact that the tsunami museum, erected to commemorate the victims of the disaster, never was finished and, due to the lack of maintenance, it is on the way to becoming a ruin soon. The project to improve the public health systems failed due to resistance inside the government agencies in charge of the reforms. Senior officers at the regional and local health offices - at the same time part-time doctors, running private clinics in the evening hours - have been the main beneficiaries of failures of the existing health system. Even as they enjoyed participating in countless workshops and conferences in Jakarta and elsewhere, legal reforms came to nothing at the end. The funds for the "Access to Justice Program" disappeared in dubious channels of civil society organizations without any visible result. To receive a birth certificate or an ID card for the poor is still in the same way difficult as before. Nowadays visitors to Aceh will hardly find any traces of all the projects in regard to government services. Instead, after international donors pulled out their stakes, Aceh became the poorhouse of Indonesia again, fully depending on subsidies of the central government. What remains from the times of donor support is an oversized airport, an unused water treatment system for desalination and hospitals, health centers or other public buildings, where the equipment was moved to private clinics or households, and of course the epidemic corruption. The windfall winners of the tsunami, who have made a fortune by leasing their Aceh premises for fancy prices to donor organizations and their staff or by offering other services, have moved in the meantime to other more prosperous regions.

But Aceh is obviously only an exception. Looking on the overall situations, since Suharto has stepped down, other parts of the country have made progress in regard to democracy as well as in economic growth. This is due to people not being afraid any more of the government, due to some brave officers at the independent anti-corruption commission, and due to judges at the constitutional court who can rely on public protests when old forces in the police or other government bodies try to obstruct their fight against corruption. The business climate also has significantly improved over the last years.

One of the reasons why this spirit has not touched Aceh so far is probably that people in Jakarta or elsewhere in Indonesia have learned to fight for their rights. By contrast, in Aceh donors have pampered intellectuals and reform-willing forces in society by offering them advisor contracts, study tours and overseas conferences. As a result their attention was drawn away from solving the real problems in a manner which would have been in line with Acehnese culture and habits. Instead of this they have been busy

with writing workshop proposals to introduce
Western ideas of good governance. Those who
have been successful doing so are not anymore in
the backwardness of Aceh. They moved with their
families to their newly purchased houses or
apartments on Jakarta, where they can enjoy
their weekends in one of the steadily growing
number of currently more than 50 shopping
malls.

Thus, Aceh donor monies have had an impact of
course, but far away from the objectives
expressed in Western good governance programs.


## VIII. Some remakes to decentralization programs in Central Africa

In contrast to Asian counties like Indonesia and
Cambodia, statehood in Africa is much more
fragile. At the beginning of the 21st century only
15 out of 48 African states (in the south of
Sahara) were judged to have functioning
governments [37] and the situation has worsened
since then. Among these states Cameroon is still
one of the most stable. [38] But as the analyses
above have demonstrated, progress in the state-
building process is still too low and the
organizational structure of the government is still
much too weak for the Western model of

---

[37] Erdmann, 2003, p. 268.
[38] Becker & Kopp, 2014 p. 22 et seq.

decentralization. Even after two decades of decentralization reforms and millions of Euros of donor support - besides heaps of legal documents and concept papers - no progress is visible on the ground. Albeit decentralization has proved to be much too complex for a country, which is probably already the most advanced in the region (inclusive the education of the population), similar programs have been launched in states far behind Cameroon.

In regard to Mali - much more backward compared with Cameroon - a donor paper, issued in 2006, stated in colorful words on colorful paper: *"The power returns to the countryside – communes, the arenas for participation and good governance."* The first chapters of the brochure praise the country for its progress in the sector of democracy and decentralization. But surprisingly on one of the following pages the same brochure starts to describe the obviously insurmountable hurdles of patrimonialism, nepotism, the corruption of the elites and in the government, the weakness of the parliament and the unreliable judiciary system.[39] These are not really signs of progress in the sector of democracy and decentralization. The conflict in Northern Mali led to the evacuation of the international staff of the decentralization project in 2012. The head of the mission of the decentralization project was apparently not really unhappy about this fact,

---

[39] GTZ - Betke, 2006.

because her counterpart on the side of the Mali government made it clear for her when she started with her job by stating: *"No illusions, you and your project are not welcome here."* Similar stories could be told about decentralization programs in Burkina Faso, where Blaise Compaoré, the most recent president, who ruled the country from 1987, was ousted from power by the popular youth upheaval of October 31, 2014, or from Niger, probably the most backward country in the region.

But no lessons have been learned from all these experiences. Even there has been an endless number of serious tribal clashes since independence of the South Sudan from the northern part of the country in 2011, and the following bloody war between Dinkes and Nuer was not surprising for observers, the program "Support for Administrative Reform and Decentralisation" (basically in place already since 2007[40]) tried *"increasing the capacities of officials in municipal administrations and .. [lay] the foundation for an on-going, regular exchange among the various administrative levels by advisory services and training programs are and promotes participatory planning and budgeting along with conflict- and gender-sensitive forms of*

---

[40] The idea to foster decentralization in Sudan derived obviously from the misunderstanding that the Western system of local autonomy is only the modern form of native tribal-based authority system (see also Aeberli, 2012).

*popular participation.*[41] While the civil conflict is still unresolved and at least 10,000 people have been killed and millions have been displaced by fighting that erupted since the conflict began,[42] the program website claims *"training courses with specific curricula have been conducted based on a needs assessment"* and *"that nearly 1,500 municipal administrative officials in all of the member states have received instruction in four-week orientation courses. Some 30 officials have been given a four-month pilot course of follow-on training."* Probably it will take some time till they are in the position to make use of their newly purchased skills.[43]

## IX. Fukuyama's End of History and Parson's evolutionary universals in society

Fukuyama, in his great book "The End of History and the last Man,"[44] has stated that it seems to be true what George W.F. Hegel, in "The Phenomenology of Mind," [45] and the Russian scholar Alexandre Kojève, [46] in interpreting Hegel's, work have asserted: History in the sense of further progress in development of underlying principles and institutions came to an end with

---

[41] Deutsche Gesellschaft für Internationale Zusammenarbeit (GIZ), kein Datum.

[42] Soi, 2014

[43] Good overview over the current political and administrative situation by Schmidt (Schmidt, 2014).

[44] Fukuyama, 1992.

[45] Hegel, 1967.

[46] Kojève, 1980 [1947].

the emergence of the liberal democracy as a political system with less contradiction that can satisfy the needs of men in a better way, is not in sight.[47] Democracy is strongly linked to the rule of law and a rational and a legal working bureaucratic system in the sense of Max Weber. Parsons has called bureaucracy, the rule of law and democratic associations evolutionary universals, [48] which means phenomena or precisely speaking results of evolution that emerge independently on several places at the world. These evolutionary universals in the social world provide their societies with major adaptive advantages over societies not developing them. A bureaucratic government system is principally more beneficial to a society than a tribal based one, and this makes it likely that a tribal society will shift to a bureaucratic government system over time. If experience about social development in the past is indicative, it seems to be certain that democracy, the rule of law and bureaucracy and good governance therefore will appear one day practically around the globe, similar to inventions like the wheel, the script or agriculture. However the question is when this will happen. Parsons has pointed to the fact that the introduction and institutionalization of evolutionary universals have often been attended with severe dislocations of the previous social

---

[47] Fukuyama, 1992, p. xii.
[48] Parsons, 1964, p. 354 et seq.

organization. [49] The hurdle for the adaptation therefore is not that the need for reforms is not understood in societies, particularly among their leaders. It is the fear of short-run losses, [50] probably not so much on the material level, but first and foremost in regard to existing values and overall concepts of the society. Therefore dissatisfaction of the population may lead to a situation, where a corrupt and reform-resisting government will be drummed out of office and replaced by actors, promising economic welfare, and democracy. But what Acemoglu and Robinson have called the "virtuous circle"[51] will frequently lead soon to the same style of government as before due to a deeply ingrained concept of leadership. Fukuyama has explained this phenomena in his book "The Origins of Social Orders" by the fact that human beings by nature gravitate towards the favoring of kinsmen and friends with whom they have exchanged favor unless strongly incentivized to do otherwise. [52] When tribal societies developed to states, this leads unavoidably to a system of patronage and nepotism. History provides many examples where societies have tried to replace this kind of system

---

[49] Parsons, 1964, p. 341.

[50] For example in the middle age aristocrats in Hungary and in Poland insisted for egoistic reasons on their autonomy right what weakened the central power of the king even in the face of the threat of external powers. This led to the defeat of their army, the occupation of their county by societies like the Mongols, which had developed a government-system with strong central power.

[51] Acemoglu & Robinson, 2012, p. 342.

[52] Fukuyama, 2011, S. 43.

with a bureaucracy that banned or limited the inheritance of public offices. The Legalism and Confucianism in China, the Ottoman Empire and the Mamluks in Egypt are probably the best known examples. But in all these cases the elites finally have been able to get rid of these restrictions. Only in Europe, where permanent warfare with armies of mercenaries forced the rulers at the end of the middle age to rise and manage huge funds, bureaucracy was established in a lasting way and formed the foundation for introducing the rule of law and democracy. [53] While this is not the place to demonstrate why this happened only in Europe and the British colonies of white settlements (Australia, New Zealand and USA, partly in South Africa and former Rhodesia), it should have become clear that developing the preconditions for a system of good governance is a complex and time-consuming process that goes far beyond the reach of any development cooperation program.

## X. Overall result

In theory decentralization can support the fight against poverty, but only in case political (democratic) decentralization will be achieved. The chance to implement the concept of political

---

[53] This was of course not the single reason but only a feature of a much more complex process. The base for the rule of law for example was probably laid in the early middle ages in Europe when individual property rights on land started to replace the old system of tribal ownership and forced the creation a system of private ownership.

decentralization in developing counties however is very low, due to the fact that it doesn't match with the prevailing social order in most of these countries. The existing social order of a society cannot be changed by the means of development cooperation of course. Western good governance concepts may have worked in East European countries which share the same culture and historic background as their Western neighbors, when they were transforming their societies from a communistic to a liberal system. But, like the Ukraine conflict shows, this essay becomes already very difficult as soon as we cross the borderline which has once separated the catholic/protestant from the orthodox world. Therefore donor support to such projects in Africa and in Asia[54] will frequently not meet the goal and will not lead to poverty alleviation. Cambodia is in this regard not a single case. The findings apply to most donor-supported good governance projects in developing countries.

---

[54] The situation in Latin America requires special consideration due to the colonial history which led to the dominance by white elites and an early independence from their weak colonial powers in the 19th Century.

## XI. Bibliography

Acemoglu, D., & Robinson, J. (2012). *Why nations fail : The origins of power, prosperity, and poverty.* New York: Crown Publishing.

Acemoglu, D., & Robinson, J. A. (2012). *Warum Nationen Scheitern - Die Ursprünge von Macht, Wohlstand und Armut.* (B. Rullkötter, Übers.) Frankfurt: S. Fischer.

Aeberli, A. (2012). *Decentralistion Hybridized - A Western Concept on its Way through South Sudan.* Geneva: Graduate Institute Publications.

Becker, P. (2014). *Dezentralisierung durch Armutsminderung in Kambodscha - Die Grenzen ambitiöser Entwicklungsvorhaben.* Berlin : LIT Verlag.

Becker, P., & Kopp, A. (2014). *Transformationsziel Demokratie. Dezentralisierung und Zivilgesellschaft in Kamerun.* Berlin: Lit-Verlag.

Bit, S. (1991). *The Warrior Heritage. A Psychological Perspective of Cambodian Trauma .* El Cerrtio: zitiert nach Karbaum, S. 150.

Brinkley, J. (18. April 2011). *Aid to Cambodia rarely reaches the people it's meant to help.* Abgerufen am 9. August 2001 von The Washington Post: http://www.washingtonpost.com/opinions/ai

d-to-cambodia-rarely-reaches-the-people-its-meant-to-help/2011/04/15/AF2JN8vD_print.html

Brinkley, J. (2011a). *Cambodia's Curse: The modern history of a troubled land.* New York: Public Affairs.

Chandler, D. (2008). *A History of Cambodia.* Chiang Mai: Silkworm Books.

Deutsche Gesellschaft für Internationale Zusammenarbeit (GIZ). (kein Datum). *GIZ.* Abgerufen am 16. Dezember 2014 von Support for Administrative Reform and Decentralisation Project description: https://www.giz.de/en/worldwide/24192.html

Eisenstadt, S. N. (1973). *Tradition, Change, and Modernity.* New York: John Wiley & Sons.

Erdmann, G. (2003). Apokalyptische Trias: Staatsversagen,Staatsverfall und Staatszerfall – strukturelle Probleme der Demokratie in Afrika. In P. Bendel, A. Croissant, & F. (. Rüb, *Demokratie und Staatlichkeit, Systemwechsel zwischen Staatlichkeit und Staatskollaps* (S. 267-292). Opladen: Leske+Budrich.

Erler, B. (2003). *Tödliche Hilfe - Bericht von meiner letzten Dienstreise in Sachen Entwicklungshilfe.* Köln: Hayit Medien.

Fukuyama, F. (1992). *The End of History and the Last Man.* New York: The Free Press.

Fukuyama, F. (2011). *The Origins of Political Order - From Perhuman Times to the*

*French Revolution*. London: Profile Books LTD.

GTZ - Betke, D. (2006). *Mali - Die Macht kehrt zurück aufs Land. Die Gemeinde als Arena für Partizipation und Gute Regierungsführung.* Eschborn: Gesellschaft für Technische Zusammenarbeit - Sektorvorhaben Mainstreaming Participation.

GTZ - Stabstelle für Evaluierung. (2009). *Programm unabhängige Evaluierung im Thema Dezentralisierung - Synthesebericht 2008.* Eschborn: Gesellschaft für Technische Zusammenarbeit.

Habermas, J. (1984). *The Theory of Communicative Action.* Boston: Beacon Press.

Hegel, G. W. (1967). *The Phenomenology of Mind,.* (J. B. Baillie, Übers.) New York: Harper and Row.

Karbaum, M. (2008). *Kambodscha unter Hun Sen - Informelle Institutionen, Politische Kultur und Herrschaftslegitimität.* Berlin: LiT Verlag Dr. W. Hopf.

Kielwein, N.-C. (2007). *Entwicklungszusammenarbeit und politische Konditionalität; Magisterarbeit an der Rheinischen Friedrich-Wilhelms-Universität, Bonn, Philosophischen Fakultät.* Abgerufen am 25. Juli 2012 von Uni-Bonn: http://www.uni-

bonn.de/~uzd007/magisterarbeiten/mag_kie
lwein.pdf

Kojève, A. (1980 [1947]). *Introduction to the Reading of Hegel. Lectures on the Phenomology of the Spirit.* Cornell: University Press.

Luco, F. (2003). *Between a tiger and a crocodile: Management of local conflicts in Cambodia. An social anthropological approach to traditional and new practices of Management of Local Conflicts in Cambodia.* Phnom Penh: UNESCO.

Manor, J. (16.-18. Dezember 1997). *The Promis and Limitation of Decentralization.* Abgerufen am 25. Juli 2012 von SDdimesions (FAO): http://www.fao.org/sd/rodirect/ROfo0019.htm

Mehler, A. (2008). Zwischen Polizeistaat und Fassadendemokratie. Eine politische Geschichte Kameruns. In K. Wertmann, & G. Schmitt, *Staatliche Herrschaft und kommunale Selbstverwaltung: Dezentralisierung* (S. 39-52). Frankfurt a.M.: Brandes & Apsel.

Merkel, W. (2010). *Systemtransformation - Eine Einführung in die Theorie und Empire der Transformationsforschung.* Wiesbaden: VS Verlag für Sozialwissenschaften.

North, D. C. (1990). *Institutions, Institutional Change and Economic Performance.*

Cambridge: Cambridge University Press.

Parsons, T. (Vol. 29, No. 3,. June 1964). Evolutionary Universals in Society. *American Sociological Review*, S. 339-357.

Roschmann, C. (2003). *Recht, Gerechtigkeit und ökonomisches Handlungsmodell.* Baden-Baden: Nomos.

Rostow, & Whiteman, W. (1960). *The Stages of Economic Growth: A Non-Communist Manifesto.* . Cambridge: Cambridge University Press.

Schmidt, R. (2014). *Failed State Südsudan?* Potsdam: WeltTrends Spezial.

Soi, C. (15. December 2014). *Al Jazerra.* Von South Sudan's civil conflict still unresolved: http://www.aljazeera.com/video/africa/2014/12/south-sudan-civil-conflict-still-unresolved-2014121585130885638.html abgerufen

Steinich, M. (1997). Dezentralisierung und Entwicklung: Licht in die entwicklungspolitische Dunkelheit. *Nord-Süd aktuel , XI Nr. 1*, 69-80.

Tata, S. (06. Februar 2013). Cameroon: Is Biya's 2035 Dream Becoming A Delusion? *ThinkAfricaPress*, http://thinkafricapress.com/cameroon/biya-2035-dream-becoming-delusion-development.

World Bank. (2012). *Cameroon - The Path to Fiscal Decentralization. Opportunities and*

*Challenges.    Report    No.    63369-CM.*
Washington: World Bank.